MW00761816

# Settlement and Progress of the Town of Bluehill, Maine

# PREFATORY NOTE.

THE following address was prepared for, and delivered on September 7th, 1886, at a clam-bake and reunion of upwards of three hundred citizens and friends upon Mill Island, at Bluehill Falls, where the settlement of the town of Bluehill, Maine, was begun April 7th, 1762.

In its preparation much time was expended, and many authorities were consulted, that it might be made worthy of the occasion; but no thought was given to the subject of its publication. Those who listened to it deemed it worthy of publication and preservation for the benefit of the youth of the town and vicinity, as well as for others interested in historical data; the request was made and acceded to, that the address should be printed by, and sold in aid of, the Ladies' Social Library of Bluehill, thereby contributing whatever might remain above the cost of publication to a needy and meritorious object.

The author acknowledges his indebtedness for facts mentioned in the address to the Town Records; the " Record " of Rev. Jonathan Fisher; the Church Records; the address of B. W. Hinckley, Esq., at the Centennial Anniversary of the Town's Settlement; the address of Rev. Stephen Thurston, at the Centennial Anniversary of the gathering of the Congregational Church; the New England Historic Genealogical Register; W. B. Sprague's Annals of the American Pulpit; John F. Pratt, M. D. of Chelsea, Mass.; contributions to the *Ellsworth American* newspaper, from papers in the Massachusetts Secretary of State's Office; Diary of Jonathan Darling, as quoted by Rev. Mr. Fisher; to Miss Abby L. Pierce, of Brookline, Mass.; to the late R. G. W. Dodge, Esq., of Bluehill; and to various other persons held in remembrance, but not mentioned here.

To the gentlemen who composed the Committee of Arrangements for the reunion and clam-bake, and to whose endeavors the pleasure and success of the occasion were largely due, the author confesses his own indebtedness, and all who were present must acknowledge theirs, and give them words of hearty commendation and praise for the success of the undertaking.

And now for this pamphlet which the author has taken much interest in writing — while he claims for it no merit as a literary production — he asks a kindly reception by an indulgent public for the facts it contains, and for the object in aid of which it is published.

R. G. F. CANDAGE.

*Brookline, Mass.,*
October 21st, 1886.

# · Order of Exercises ·

---

## DINNER.

### BASKET PICNIC.

BAKED CLAMS.                    GREEN CORN.

COFFEE.

### GROUP PHOTOGRAPHED.

### Singing.

"AULD LANG SYNE."

By the Assembly, led by CHARLES C. CLOUGH, Esq.

### Address.

By R. G. F. CANDAGE, Esq., of Brookline, Mass.

A Native of Bluehill.

### Singing.

"MY COUNTRY 'TIS OF THEE."

By the Assembly.

### Benediction.

By the REV. L. S. TRIPP.

# COMMITTEE OF ARRANGEMENTS.

Dr. Rufus P. Grindle,
Mr. Augustus C. Peters,
Mr. Augustus N. Osgood,
Mr. Alfred C. Osgood,
Mr. Thomas S. Osgood,
Mr. George Morse,
Mr. Charles C. Clough,
Mr. Wilford E. Grindle,
Mr. Brooks A. Gray,
Mr. David H. Allen,

Mr. Irving S. Candage,
Mr. Roscoe Lord,
Mr. George R. Adams,
Mr. Eugene A. Stevens,
Mr. Austin Stevens,
Mr. Frank J. Dodge,
Mr. Seth K. Hinkley,
Mr. James H. Morse,
Mr. Jonathan Stover,
Mr. George Osgood.

# ADDRESS.

———————

*Fellow Townsmen and Friends, Ladies and Gentlemen :*

WE have assembled here to-day to meet and greet
each other in social converse, to partake of the repast
which kind friends have provided for the occasion, and
to recount some of the events which have transpired
in the history of the town of Bluehill, the first settlement having been made upon this spot.

In the study of history there is much to be learned
which may be useful to us. From it we may draw lessons of wisdom to aid and encourage us in well-doing ;
and from it we may learn lessons of warning, which, if
heeded, will point out to us the rocks and shoals upon
which our barque may be stranded on the voyage of
life.

We are taught in the Book of books " To honor our
father and our mother, that our days may be long in
the land ; " and in what way can we give them higher
honor than by a study of the history of their lives, as
recorded in their acts, and by profiting by the good examples they set for us to follow.

It has been with these purposes in view that I have prepared this address, to which I invite your kind and indulgent attention.

One hundred and twenty-four years ago last April a small vessel entered the waters of Bluehill Bay, steered for these shores, and made a landing upon the island where we are now assembled. No friendly eye was fixed upon her approach; no hospitable hand was extended to greet her adventurous crew as they landed. The coast and country were covered with a dense growth of forest trees, in which roamed wild beasts and savage men. There was not a habitation for civilized man to be found in this region; the nearest being at Bagaduce, now Castine, which could only be reached by a long and circuitous route by water.

The crew of the little craft proved to be Joseph Wood and John Roundy, good men and true, from Beverly, Mass., who came here to make a home for themselves and their families in the wilderness, and to lay the foundations of a settlement, which, by their efforts, and by the aid of those who followed their adventurous lead, grew into this beautiful and prosperous town, as we shall see, when we examine the records of the settlement, the town, and the churches.

People wonder why this spot should have been chosen for the first settlement. But the reason seems to me to be plain, that they chose it because it was an island, and afforded better security from the intrusion of wild beasts and wild men, than the main land.

Here the summer of 1762 was spent by Mr. Wood and Mr. Roundy, in erecting log-houses, felling trees to make a clearing, and in getting out staves with which they loaded their little craft; and also in forming plans for the permanent settlement of the place.

In the autumn they returned to Beverly, and there spent the winter. The next year, 1763, they brought their families here; each family consisting of husband, wife, and six children.

Joseph Wood was in the full vigor of manhood, being 42 years of age, and his wife, Ruth Haskell, one year younger. Their children were Israel, 19 years old; Mary, 15; Joseph, 12; Ruth, 10; Robert Haskell, 7; and Joanna was 3.

John Roundy was six years younger than Mr Wood, he being 36 years old, and his wife, Elizabeth Rea, was 34. Their children were Mary, 15; Elizabeth, 12; Hannah, 10; Charity, 8; Anne, 5; and Emma, the baby, less than a year old.

These were the persons who planted the infant settlement of the town, and who contributed largely to the success it met with, up to, and even beyond, the date of its incorporation. The descendants of Mr. Wood, who bear his name, and also those who bear other names, are numerous in the town to-day; while the name of Roundy, so far as I have been able to ascertain, has become extinct here; although there are many descendants of his, bearing other names, residents of the town and vicinity.

He who addresses you is a lineal descendant of John Roundy, through Hannah, his daughter, who married James Candage, Jr., (formerly Cavendish), April 13, 1775; and through their son, Samuel Roundy Candage, born Jan. 15, 1781, who was his father.

The third family of the new settlement was formed by the marriage of Col. Nathan Parker, with Mary, eldest daughter of Joseph Wood, on Dec. 20, 1765. Col. Parker was from Andover, Mass., and was one of the provincial troops at the siege and fall of Louisburg.

The fourth family was Mr. Samuel Foster's, of Andover, who came in May, 1765. It is said they did not remain long.

The fifth family was that of Nicholas Holt, from Andover, who came May 27, 1765.

The sixth family was that of Jonathan Darling, also from Andover, whose wife and one child came with her father, Nicholas Holt, May 27, 1765. Mr. Darling's second son, Jonathan, was the first English child born in the town, Oct. 17, 1765. The Holt family lived in a house which stood very nearly on the spot now occupied by the house of Mr. Albert R. Conary.

The first white female child born in the town was Edith, daughter of Joseph and Mary Wood, born Aug. 3, 1766. The Wood family moved from this island to a house which was erected on the opposite side of the road, from where the school house now stands, at the head of the cove.

The seventh family was that of Mr. Benjamin York. It is recorded of them that they made but a short stay in town. By the assignment of proprietary lots of land, Benjamin York was assigned the lot of 80 acres fronting the Falls, on the Neck side, which he is recorded to have held in quiet possession and enjoyment, on Nov. 1, 1769.

The eighth family was that of Mr. Ezekiel Osgood, who came from Andover, Mass., Nov. 6, 1765. Just where Mr. Osgood and family located I have not been able to learn.

The ninth family was that of Mr. Thomas Coggins, from Beverly, who came Dec. 27, 1765. The name of "Coggin Hill" yonder, fixes the spot where they located, and also fixes the family name in the town as long as that hill shall last.

Others followed in 1766, and among them was James Candage and family, who settled on the Neck. He was the ancestor of the Candages of this town and vicinity.

The following petition is important, in so far as it fixes the date of the coming to town of the persons named therein :

BLUEHILL BAY, June 17th, 1784.

This is to certify that John Peters of the Town aforesaid this day was chose by the Inhabitants of this Town to represent the true State of the Proprietors and Settlers on Said Township to the Committe chosen by the General Court of the Massachusetts State to receive and examin the Clames of Land In the County of Lincoln (&c. &c.)

| Date of Proprietors' Settlem't | | Date of Proprietors' Settlem't | |
|---|---|---|---|
| Joseph Wood, . . . . | 1762 | Obed Johnson, . . . . | 1769 |
| Nathan Parker, . . . | 1764 | Jon'a Clay, . . . . . | 1769 |
| Jonah Dodge, . . . . | | Elizabeth Brown, widow,. | 1770 |
| Jonathan Darling, . . . | 1765 | Peter Parker, . . . . | 1765 |
| Peter Parker, jr. . . . | 1765 | Joshua Parker, . . . . | |
| Nathan Parker, jr. . . . | | Joseph Parker, . . . . | |
| Ezekiel Osgood, jr. . . | 1765 | John Roundy, . . . . | 1762 |
| Phineas Osgood, . . . | 1774 | Jos'a Titcomb, . . . . | 1769 |
| Joseph Wood, jr. . . . | | Joshua Titcomb, jr. . . | 1767 |
| Joshua Horton, . . . . | 1768 | Stephen Titcomb, . . . | 1765 |
| Benj'n Friend, . . . . | 1774 | David Carleton, . . . | |
| John Dodge, . . . . | 1774 | Moses Carleton, . . . | |
| Ezekiel Osgood, . . . | | Michael Carleton, . . . | |
| Robert Parker, . . . . | | Samuel Parker, . . . . | |
| Thomas Coggin, . . . | 1765 | James Candige, . . . | 1766 |
| Elisha Dodge, . . . . | 1774 | John Peters, . . . . . | 1765 |
| John Peters, jr. . . . , | 1765 | Nicholas Holt, . . . . | |
| Marble Parker, . . . . | 1764 | John Osgood. . . . . | |

| Settlers | Settled in | Settlers | Settled in |
|---|---|---|---|
| Israel Wood, . . . . | 1776 | Christopher Osgood, . . | 1774 |
| Daniel Osgood, . . . . | 1776 | Ebene'r Hinkley, . . . | |
| Robert Haskell Wood, . | 1776 | Jon'a Darling, jr. . . . | 1776 |
| James Candige, jr. . . | 1766 | Jon'a Day, . . . . . | 1766 |
| John Candige, . . . . | 1782 | Mathias Vickery, . . . | 1776 |
| John Randall, . . . . | 1768 | Susannah Hinkley, wid. . | 1766 |
| Joseph Candige, . . . | 1767 | Henry Carter, . . . . | 1783 |
| James Day, . . . . . | 1766 | James Carter, . . . . | 1781 |
| Thomas Carter, . . . | 1776 | Lydia Day, widow,. . . | 1766 |
| Nathan Osgood, . . . | 1776 | Nath'l Cushing, . . . | 1778 |
| Nicholas Holt, . . . . | 1775 | Jedediah Holt, . . . . | 1778 |
| John Roundy, jr.. . . | 1783 | Joshua Horton, jr. . . | 1782 |
| Josiah Coggin, . . . . | 1782 | | |

36 of the above — 7 of them, minors, all sons of Proprietors who are on ye ground except Steph Titcomb, whose father has done ye duty on his right.

No minor has his name.

Captain Joseph Wood & Sons and John Roundy came and settled at Bluehill bay before the land was either granted or layed out &c &c &c.

These early settlers were men and women, hardy and robust by nature, who undertook to plant new homes, rear and support families on the hard soil of this town, far away from the social, educational, and Christian privileges they had enjoyed in Massachusetts. I have frequently been asked, as doubtless many of you have been, why they came here to a climate so uninviting and to a new country. My reply has been, they were desirous of forming a new community, perhaps an ideal one; so they came to Maine, there being no Great West then to go to. They saw the fine timber with which the land was covered; in that their Yankee shrewdness discovered a profit, and having a realizing sense of the beautiful, they saw what every one else has seen who has visited this town, the charm of its situation, its sparkling bay, its inlets, its shores, its landscape of hill, dale, and plain; they were pleased with it, and the testimony of a century and a quarter is " that the place is beautiful to look upon." They were the persons needed for the times and the place, and right worthily and successfully did they exert their energies to fulfill their mission. We are here to-day to review, very briefly, the success they achieved, to admire the persistency with which they subdued the forest, converted the wilderness into fruitful fields, and erected homes of comfort. They could not do this without great hardships and privations. Their stock of provisions failed them; they subsisted upon clams, fish and wild game. And when, by dint of hard labor, they harvested a little Indian corn, they parched it over the fire, pounded it into meal with pestle and mortar, and baked it on boards in front of their wood-fires. The tide-mill near by this spot was erected in 1765, three years after the families of Joseph Wood and John Roundy came here. This I suppose was a mill for sawing lumber; in what year the grist-mill was built I have found no exact data to determine, but probably about the same time.

The first notification for a town meeting on record was dated " Number five, Feb. ye 20, Anno Domeney, 1767," and was signed by Joseph Wood, John Roundy, and Nicholas Holt, and contained the following articles : —

Viz. 1. To Chuse a moderator for said Meating.
" 2. To Chuse a Clarck for the year Insewing.
" 3. To see if they will agree to work one Day for a fense in A Burying Place, and to act on aney other afairs that May Be thought Proper.

The " *Meating* " was held " March ye 2, 1767," and chose Lieut. Nicholas Holt, Moderator, John Roundy, Town Clerk, John Roundy, Jonathan Darling, and Benjamin York, Com. (or Selectmen.)

Voted that the Township shall be called "Newport." Voted to clear a Burying Place and fence it one Day. Voted that if aney one Cut on aney ones Lott that is Laid Outt, without leave, he shall lose his Labor and his stuff. Voted that if aney Man shall find aney Lumber Cut on Their Lott, they shall carry it of.

The second "*Meating*" was held, "Newport Apriell ye 6, 1767."

1. Lieut. Nicholas Holt Moderator.
2. Voted that they would have their Lots put on Record and who they lay a Gainst.
3. Voted that they would Raise a Tax of Ten Shillings on the Poles, to be paid into the hands of the Town Clarck to Defray the Charge for the Year Ensuing.
4. Voted that they would have the time of their settling on Record, and who was the first settlers and so on.

March ye 7, 1768. The Town met at the house of Ensign Joseph Wood. Chose Lieut. Nicholas Holt, Moderator, John Roundy, Town Clarck, John Roundy, Nathan Parker and Jonathan Darling, Com. (or Selectmen.)

1. Voted that they would Rais Money for to hire a person to preach the Gospel to us and for to pay for his Board.

In the notice for this "meating" they say "So that we may not bring up our children like the Heathen."

2. Voted to chuse a Comitte for to provide a Man for to preach to us.

JOHN ROUNDY  
. NATHAN PARKER } Comt.  
JONATHAN DARLING

3.  Voted on the Poynt if we can get the house for Pub-
    lick Worship.
4.  Voted to clear a Rhode from here to Pronobscutt.
5.  Voted to chuse a Comitte.
6.  Voted to chuse five men for a Comitte.

$$
\left.\begin{array}{l}
\text{SAMUEL FOSTER} \\
\text{ISRAEL WOOD} \\
\text{ROBERT PARKER} \\
\text{ENSIGN JOSEPH WOOD} \\
\text{AND JOHN ROUNDY}
\end{array}\right\} \text{Comt.}
$$

## At the Town meeting held "March ye 6th 1769,"

John Peters was chosen Town Clerk, and John Peters,
Jeremiah Cobburn and Benjamin York Com. or Selectmen.
Capt. Joshua Horton, Town Treasurer.

Voted to raise 150 [probably dollars] by subscription to Defray the Charge of Preaching.

Voted to chuse a Committy to see that the Gospel is
Preached to us.  Joshua Herrick, Ensign Joseph Wood and
Lieut. Nicholas Holt, Comt.

Voted to repare the old Meeting House for a place of Pub-
lick Worship for the Year Insuing.

Voted to chuse a Committy to lay out Roads where they
shall think proper to convean the Town on this side the Salt
Pond.  Ensign Joseph Wood, Jonathan Darling and Robert
Parker, Comt.

Voted a Committy to lay out Roads where they think
proper on the Neck.  Jonathan Darling, John Roundy and
Benjamin York, Comt.

Voted to *except* what was done, then ajourned till the 27th
of March.  At the *ajourned* meeting, March 27, John
Roundy was chosen to be the Surveyor of Lumber.

Another *meating* of the Town was held April 24, 1769.

Voted the first Munday in may to repare the Meeting House.

Voted that Ensign Joseph Wood, Lieut. Nicholas Holt and Mr. Joshua Herrick should be Collectors.

Voted that Jeremiah Coburn should be the man to see that the Boards are procured for the Meeting House.

Voted that Ensign Joseph Wood should be the man to see that the Glass and Nails are Provided for to repare the old Meeting House.

Voted that they would clear a Road half way from the head of the Bay to No. Six (Surry.)

Voted that Capt. Peter Parker, Ensign Joseph Wood and Ensign John Roundy should be a Committy to Look out said Road.

Then follows a vote which shows that the men of that day were ready to grapple with great questions.

Voted that they would fence in the Township !

Here follows a record of laying out lots of land on the Neck, and assigning them to those in quiet and peaceful possession and enjoyment.

NEWPORT, Nov. 1st, 1769.

From the Neck of land in this Township, laid out into Eighty Acres Lots, Beginning at the fore falls and running from thence upon the shore Southward about 150 Rods to a Spring, and from thence across the Neck, such a course as shall Give eighty Acres upon the end of the Neck : — this Lot of land then being in Quiet and Peaceable Possession and Enjoyment of Benjamin York of said Town.

Secondly — beginning at said Spring and laying out seven more lots on said Neck, each being Sixty Rods wide on the front and running a Crost the Neck over to the Salt Pond, such a course as shall give eighty Acres to Each Lot.

Mr. John Roundy then being in the Quiet and Peaceable Possession and Enjoyment of the first of these Lots of Land joining upon Mr. Benjamin York.

Mr. Jonathan Day was assigned the second of these Lots of Land.

Mr. James Cavendish, [the great grandfather of the speaker], was assigned Lots three and four.

Mr. Ebenezer Hinckley was assigned Lot five.

Mr. James Day Lot six, and Mr. John York Lot seven.

I find no other assignment of lands to the settlers in the first book of Records of the Town, which Record ends Dec. 7, 1801.

At the meeting held March 5, 1770, John Peters was chosen Town Clerk, Peter Parker, Dudley Carlton, and Jonathan Day, Selectmen.

Voted to have 3 or 4 Months' Preaching for the Summer Coming — to raise the Money to Defray the Charge of Preaching by Subscription — Peter Parker, Dudley Carlton and Jeremiah Cobborn be the Committy men to Provide a Person to Preach the Gospel to us and likewise to gether the Rates.

Voted that the course should be kept open at the Mill Endeavor, and that Peter Parker, Joseph Wood, and John Roundy be the Committy to keep it clear.

Voted to work on the Burying Yard the 25th of April.

Voted that Capt. Joshua Horton should receive pay for buying the Town Books.

Voted to build some thing of a Battery on Mill Point by the first of May next.

Voted Ensign Dudley Carlton and Lieut. John Roundy, Surveyors of Lumber.

Voted to go over to Long Island to begin to clear, the second Day of April.

Voted to Joyn with No. 4 People to hire a minister, if they could agree upon it hereafter.

At the March meeting in 1771, John Peters was chosen Clerk, and Ensg. Dudley Carlton, Mr. Jonathan Day and John Peters, Selectmen.

At the March meeting in 1772, Joseph Wood was Moderator. John Peters was chosen Town Clerk, and Joseph Wood, Robert Parker, and John Peters, Selectmen.

Voted to lay out a Road from Mr. Osgood's to Mr. H's, and the meeting was then ajourned to first Monday in may at three o'Clock in the afternoon.

The annual March meeting ajourned to may 4th, then met, and

Voted that there should be no fish taken above the Mill Called Carltons Mill; and that no fish be taken at Carltons Mill on Saturday, Sunday, Tuesday, Thursday, for the year Insuing.

Voted that no Bevor be taken within this Township within the term of six months from the Date hereof.

Voted, if any man shall find any Trap upon any Pond or Stream within this Township, and will bring it to the Town Clerk, shall have a Dollar reward, and the Trap to his own.

Att a meating of the Inhabitants of the Town of New Port when mett att the Meating hous March ye 1, 1773,

1. Lieutt. Nicholas Holt Being Chosen Moderator.
   They Ajourned the meating to the house of Capt. Joseph Wood.

2. Voted that they would Chuse Town oficers by handey vote.

3. Made Choyse of John Roundy as Town Clarck.

4. John Roundy, Joshua horton and Nathan Parker as Select Men for the Year Ensuing.

5. James Candage, Thomas Coggen and Ezekiel Osgood as Survaers of The high ways.

6. John Roundy, Joshua Horton Survaers of Lumber.

7. Ezekiel Osgood, Israel Wood and James Candage as a Committe For to Provide a Man for to Preach to us and Gether the Muney subscribed for to Pay him when his Labour is Dun.

8. Voted for to send a Protition to see If they could Gett the Town Incorporated.

9. The meating is A Journed untill the twelft Day of Apriel Next att fore o'Clock in the After noon att Capt. Joseph Woods hous In Said Town.

Apriel ye 12 Day 1773.

Anniuel March Meeting that was ajourned untill This Day Is further A Journed Until the Tweney six Day of May Next Insuing att 2 o'Clock in the After noon att the Meating Hous in Sd Town.

May ye 20 Day 1773. When mett to Gether then made Choyse of Mr. Ezekiel Osgood As a Seuar of the high ways

in Roome of Mr. Jonathan Darling for Bluehill Ward. the
Aniuel March Meating that was Ajourned Untill this Day Is
Desold.

Att a Meating of the Inhabitants of. When Mett of the
Town of Newport March ye 7 1774.

1. Made Choice of Lt. Nicholas Holt as Moderator.
2. Voted that they would chuse Town Ofisers By handey
   vote.
3. Made choice of John Roundy as Town Clarck.
4. John Roundy, Joshua Horton and Nathan Parcker,
   Selectmen.
5. John Roundy, Joshua Horton Souars of Lumber.
6. Suares of High Ways. Ebenezer Hinskley for Royal
   Rode, ward; Thomas Coggins for the Town Ward,
   or District, and Zebediah Shattuck for Bluehill
   Ward or District.
7. Voted that they would have the Gospel preached with
   them.
8. Mr. Ezeekel Osgood is Chosen a Warden for the year
   Insueing.
9. Mr. Jonathan Day, Mr. Joseph Wood juner and David
   Carlton Corlectors for the Year Insuing.
10. Voted that they pay what they subscribe for the Year
    Insuing on the 25th Day of May.
11. The Meating is Ajourned untill the 28th Day of this
    Instant March att 3 o'Clock in the After Noon att
    Lieut. Holts, Inholders.

## NEWPORT March ye 28 Day 1774.

1. The Annival March Meating is Untill 28th of March
   when Mett.

2. Voted that the Commites Back from Year to Year from the Beginning of the Commites att this Town or Place Shall Bring in their Acompts to A Commitey when they Shall Be Called for, In order for a Setelment.

3. Voted that they would Clear the fish corse Through Carltons Mill and Mr. Wood's and Titcomb's Dam, for the Elwives to have a corse.

4. The Annieul March Meating Is A Jornd Untill the Tenth Day of May Next Insuing att 10 oClock in the Morning att Capt. Joseph Woods.

NEWPORT May ye 10, 1774.

When Mett Ajourned the Meating Untill the 25 Day of May Next Insuing.

NEWPORT ye 25 Day 1774.

When Mett By Vartey of a Vote of the Inhabitants of the Town, Voted that they would Chuse a Committ For to Receive the Acompts of the Committes when Brought In from this Date Back to the Year 1769.

JOHN ROUNDY
AND JOHN PETERS } A Committ.

For to Meat on the 29th Day of June Next Insuing att Eight O'Clock in the Morning att Lieut. Nicholas Holts Inholder In Said Town.

NEWPORT June 29 Day 1774.

When Mett and None of the Committes Apeared So we Desolved the Anniual Meating.

NEWPORT March 6th 1775.

Made Choice of Capt Joseph Wood as Moderator, John Peters as Town Clerk, Lieut. Nicholas Holt, Capt. Joseph

Wood, and John Peters as Selectmen. Capt. Joseph Wood, Joshua Horton, Zebediah Shattuck Survairs of Lumber.

Capt. Peter Parker, Lieut. Nicholas Holt and Mr. Jonathan Day as Survairs of highways.

Voted to work two days on highways.

Made Choice of Mr. Thomas Coggins, Mr. Jonathan Day, Juner, and Ezekiel Osgood, Juner, to provide a minister for this season.

At the adjourned Meeting, April 3, 1775.

Made Choice of Joseph Wood, Nicholas Holt and Thomas Coggins as a Committy to treat with Number four People conserning hiring a minister together this Season.

Voted to ajourn to the house of Mr. David Carlton the 2d monday in may to see Something abought making the hour Something better, the People are to meet at Eight o'Clock in the morning. The Disturbance Between Brittan and America Prevented the meeting in According to Ajournment.

NEWPORT, July 17, 1775.

Att a Meeting of the Freeholders and other Inhabitants of the Town aforesaid.

Voted that Lieut. Nicholas Holt, Joshua Horton and John Peters be Delegates to meet Delegates of other Towns, Islands and Districts, at the house of Mr. John Been's of Frenchman's Bay, 20th inst., to Act on any thing they shall think Proper on said Day.

But as to whether they met or acted upon anything " Proper " or otherwise, the record is silent.

LINCOLN S.S. To Joseph Wood, Sir Agreable to a Resolve of the Great and General Court of the Colony of Massachusetts Bay held at Water town febr. 15 1776, this is to order and Direct you to warn a meeting of the Inhabitants of Bluehill Bay to meet at the house of Joseph Wood aforesaid on Thursday the Twenty Eight of March at one oclock in the After Noon then and there to Chuse a Committy of Inspection Correspondence and Safety agreable to Said Resolve.

Given under my hand and Seal at Majebeguiduce this Ninth Day of March Anno Domini 1776.

JOHN BAKEMAN Justice Peace.

N.B.

It is expected by the General Court that no Person will be chosen into any office, but such as have ever been real friend to the united Colonies. Pursuant to this warrant I do notifie all the Inhabitants of Bluehill Bay to meet at the time and Place above mentioned. Mach 28 1776.

JOSEPH WOOD.

This is the first time Bluehill Bay is mentioned in the Book of Records. After this Bluehill Bay is the name by which the place is designated until October, 1788, when the Town

Voted to Desire the Court to Call the name of this Town when Incorporated by the Name of Bluehill.

The meeting in accordance with John Bakeman's and Joseph Wood's notice was held March 28, 1776, and

Chose Joseph Wood Moderator, Joshua Horton, Nathan Parker and David Carlton a Committy of Correspondence. John Peters, Zebediah Shattuck and John Roundy a Committy of Safety.

At the Annual Meeting March 3, 1777, Joseph Wood was chosen Moderater; John Peters, Town Clerk; Joseph Wood,

Peter Parker, and Zebediah Shattuck, Selectmen; Joseph Wood, Peter Parker and John Roundy, a Committy of Safety.

March 2, 1778, Joseph Wood chosen Moderater; John Peters, town Clerk; Nicholas Holt, Zebediah Shattuck and Robert Parker, Selectmen; John Roundy, Nathan Parker and John Peters, a Committy of Safety.

March 1, 1779, Joseph Wood, Moderater, John Peters, Town Clerk; Joseph Wood, John Peters and Zebediah Shattuck, Selectmen and Committy of Safety; David Carlton, Nathan Parker and James Candage, Surveyors of highways. Voted to lay out a road from Mr. Hinckley's to No. 4; and another over Beach Hill, where the Selectmen think most convenient. The meeting then disolved.

Then this statement is entered upon the records:

By reason of the War we have had no Meetings from the year 1779 to 1784.

This brings us to the end of the war of the Revolution.

At a meeting of the town held Oct. 9, 1788, John Roundy, Moderator: —

Voted to send a Petition to Court to see if they will remit our taxes, and to Desire the Court to Call the name of this Town when incorporated by the name of Bluehill. "

On the 30th day of January, 1789, the town was incorporated by act of the Massachusetts Legislature, and received the name of Bluehill, which it has ever since held. In the same year Sedgwick was incorporated Jan. 12, the 59th town to be chartered in the

District of Maine, Islesboro the 61st, Bluehill 62d, Deer Isle 63d, Trenton 65th, Gouldsborough 66th, Sullivan 67th, Mt. Desert 68th and Vinalhaven 71st. All of the above were then within the County of Hancock.

At the March Meeting, 1789, John Roundy, Moderator; John Peters, Town Clerk; Jonathan Darling, Joshua Horton and Phinehas Osgood, Selectmen; Edward Carlton, Robert Parker, John Roundy, Phinehas Osgood, and Jonathan Clay, Surveyors of Highways; Joseph Wood and Joshua Horton, Surveyors of Lumber; Phinehas Osgood and Joseph Wood, Surveyors of the Fish Course. These were the officers of the town the first year of its incorporation.

Voted to give one days [work] towards clearing the fish course round the West end of Mr. Carlton's Mill Dam, at notice of the Surveyors.

Carlton's Mill was afterwards known as Allen's Mill.

Voted to go the fifth day of May to clear a road from Bluehill to No. 6, (now Surry) : —

Having thus examined the Records from the first settlement to the incorporation of the town, let us now examine briefly its church history. The early settlers of Bluehill had been reared in Massachusetts, under the influence of the schools and religious institutions and Puritan preachers of their time. They brought with them a loving regard for the Bible, the Sabbath, the

Christian ministry, and their value in the training of their families. So we find them early taking steps to secure the preaching of the Gospel, " in order, " as they phrased it, " that their children should not grow up like the heathen." Six years after the first landing, they voted " to raise money to hire a person for to preach the Gospel to us and for to pay his board." Ten years from the time the settlement began, October 7th, 1772, the first church was gathered, consisting of fourteen members. The March meeting of 1772 was notified to assemble at the meeting house; so it appears that they had a place for public worship in the vicinity of the tide mills at this early date. They were assisted in the service of the church by the Rev. Daniel Little, a missionary from Wells, Me.

The nearest church, at the time this was formed, was at Phippsburg, and the next nearest at Brunswick. The Bluehill Church was the Twenty-fourth Congregational Church in the District of Maine, but whether there were any of other denominations I have not been able to ascertain. The confession of faith and covenant was signed by eight men, and the wives of six of them were voted into the privileges and under the watch of the church. From the founding of the church in 1772 to the coming of Rev. Jonathan Fisher in 1794, there were twelve different ministers who preached and labored with them.

The house of worship at the Falls did not long meet the wants of the church. In 1790 the town passed a vote in regard to the new meeting house. It will be remembered that at that early day, the town was the parish and the parish the town, hence the action taken by the town in regard to matters of public worship. In 1791 the former vote was reconsidered, and another location chosen, and the size of the new house fixed at 50 by 40 feet, and one hundred pounds voted for building it. In 1792 another slight change was made in the location, and a vote was passed dividing the town into classes for building the house. At a meeting in 1792 " the Selectmen were empowered to procure one barrel of rum, also molasses and sugar enough for framing and raising the meeting house."

It was said that every man, woman, and child in town attended this raising. A wag was uncharitable enough to suggest that the reason they were all there was on account of that barrel of rum. At any rate there has doubtless been a considerable change in the temperance sentiment of the town since that time.

July 13, 1796, Rev. Jonathan Fisher was ordained, and became the pastor of the Bluehill Congregational Church. The meeting house was not finished at that. time, as the ordination services are said to have been held in an open field, nearly opposite the present Town Hall; the Rev. Peter Powers, of Deer Isle, preached the sermon.

The terms of Mr. Fisher's settlement were: a minister's lot of three hundred acres of wild land, two hundred dollars in cash, and a barn 30 by 40 feet as a

settlement.  His annual salary was two hundred dollars
in cash, the clearing of five acres of land, and cutting
and hauling fifteen cords of wood for the first ten years.
After that two hundred dollars, and thirty cords of wood
yearly, with a vacation of five Sabbaths each year.

The whole of his salary did not amount to more than
three hundred dollars, yet on this sum he lived comfortably and reared a family.  But he and his good wife
knew how to economize.

In 1797, the year after the pews were sold at
public auction, it is recorded that there was a great
revival in this place, and in the churches at Sedgwick,
Deer Isle, and Mt. Desert.  The result at Bluehill
was that fifty-seven persons joined the church under
the pastoral care of the Rev. Jonathan Fisher.  In
1804-5 a change came over some of the people of this
town and vicinity in regard to the ordinance of baptism.
The church at Sedgwick, then under the pastoral care
of the Rev. Daniel Merrill, an educated and devout
man, met with this change, and with their pastor were
baptised by immersion, and were formed into a Baptist
Church.  The Rev. Mr. Merrill was reordained as its
pastor, and continued to preach in the same house and
to the same people.

In 1805 twenty-eight members of Mr. Fisher's church
at Bluehill seceded, being dissatisfied with their baptism.  February 13, 1806, seventeen of them were
formed into a Baptist Church, and held meetings by
themselves.  Others followed, until forty-seven mem-

bers of Mr. Fisher's church withdrew and united with the Baptist Church.

These are said to have been days of great trial to Mr. Fisher, as nearly all of the seceding members had been converted and brought into the church under his preaching. These were days when denominational feeling was unyielding and rancorous; but it is said, to the honor of Mr. Fisher, that he was not known to express an unkind word against, or reflection upon, any Christian brother for the course he had taken; and he was known to pray fervently and devoutly for the blessing of God on the new church which had sprung from among his own people.

Let us all rejoice that at this day, Christians, though differing in forms of church government, yet holding to the essential points of the Gospel, may live together in the same community in Christian charity and love, and respect each other as brethren.

In 1816 there was another revival, many were converted, forty-seven were added to Mr. Fisher's church, and a much larger number were gathered into the Baptist Church. In the year 1834 another revival was the means of adding forty-two to the Congregational Church, and also a large number to the Baptist Church.

In the year 1837, Mr. Fisher, being then advanced in years, gave place to a younger man, Mr. Albert Cole, to be the pastor, after a long and faithful service of over forty years in the church. Mr. Fisher was a graduate of Harvard College, came to Bluehill when the town was small, labored forty-one years, and left upon the people the stamp of his piety and individuality, which aided greatly in making this an intelligent and intellectual community.

It may be a new and interesting fact to some present to learn that Father Fisher was licensed to preach in Brookline, Mass., the town where I reside, and that he was a college friend of the Rev. John Pierce, D.D., who, for nearly fifty years, was the settled minister over the first Parish of that town (Unitarian), and that between them existed a life-long friendship.

Very largely through his influence, the Bluehill Academy was incorporated in 1803, over which he watched and labored to promote its prosperity and usefulness as a seat of learning, not only for this town, but for the vicinity. That it has done much for the intellectual cultivation of the people, and given to them a standing as a cultivated, intelligent community, no one will deny who is conversant with its history.

The church which was built in the last century, after much planning and with much sacrifice by the early settlers, was modeled after the Old South Church in Boston, as I have been informed, having square pews, a gallery round three sides, a high pulpit with flights of steps leading up to it, and sounding board over it. In summer, when the windows were open during service, the wind would move the sounding-board, which was suspended by a rope from the ceiling, and, as a boy, I

have looked at it and wondered what would be the con-
sequence if the rope should break, and the sounding-
board should fall upon the head of the then venerable
Father Fisher. Perhaps my mind ought to have been
occupied with other things, but I found that, as a boy,
my thoughts were not under proper control, as doubtless many of more mature years have learned in their
experience.

The sounding-board held its place, however, until
the first Sabbath of 1841, nearly four years after the
pastoral care of the church had passed into the hands
of Rev. Albert Cole, when the building was totally
destroyed by fire. The present Congregational church
edifice was erected in 1843.

The Baptist Church in this town was formed Feb.
13th, 1806, consisting of thirty members (including
those who came from the Congregational Church,) at
its organization. In 1807 its members sent the following petition to the Massachusetts General Court : —

To the Honorable Senate and House of Representatives
of the Commonwealth of Massachusetts in General Court assembled ; — The Petition of the Subscribers, Inhabitants of
the Town of Blue Hill, humbly Show that we belong to the
denomination of Christians known by the name of Baptists,
and that we have for almost two years kept up and Supported
the Worship of God among ourselves, neither disturbing or
Interfering with others who do not believe as we do : and notwithstanding we do not, nor cannot Conscientiously attend on
the preaching of the Congregational Minister Settled in this

Town, we are Taxed and Compelled to pay towards his Stated Salary, which we conceive to be a burden grievous to be borne, and Contrary to the principle which ought to govern all the professed followers of the Lord Jesus Christ. We therefore wish (in order to be delivered from this burden and that we may have our own money to Support such a preached Gospel as we believe to be agreeable to the word of God) to be incorporated into a Baptist Society, with all the privileges with other Religious Incorporated Societies and as in duty bound will ever pray. Signed

| | | |
|---|---|---|
| JEREMIAH STOVER | PETER PARKER, JR. | SAMUEL MORSE |
| JOSHUA PARKER | SETH KIMBALL | MARTHA FRIEND |
| SPENCER TREWORGY | ISAIAH HINKLEY | HENRY DORITY |
| WILLIAM JOHNSON | JOHN BURNHAM | JOHN OSGOOD |
| JOHN CANDAGE | BENJAMIN BUNKER | ANDREW WOOD |
| BENJAMIN FRIEND | PHILLIP HEWINS | ASA CLOUGH |
| AMOS ALLEN | JOHN ROUNDY | EBENEZER HINKLEY |
| ISAAC INGALLS | ABRAHAM TREWORGY | |

BLUEHILL, Dec 24, 1807.

What answer, if any, the General Court returned to this petition I have not learned.

The first pastor of this church was John Roundy, the son of John Roundy the first settler, and a younger brother of the grandmother of him who now addresses you.

He held the pastoral care and charge of the church from 1809 to March, 1821, when he was dismissed and became pastor of the church in Penobscot; later he was employed as a missionary by the Maine Baptist Home Missionary Society, and spent the remainder of his days of usefulness in that service. He lived to a great age, being 90 or upwards at the time of his death.

The Bluehill Baptist Church had a steady and healthy growth, numbering upon its records in 1816, ten years after it was gathered, two hundred members that were then, or had been connected with it.

The Baptist Church edifice, I am informed, was erected in the year 1817.

In August, 1825, a Baptist Church was formed on Bluehill Neck, consisting of fourteen members who had withdrawn from the church at Bluehill for that purpose. The present church on the Neck is a Free Baptist Church, organized some twenty-five years ago; the church founded in 1825 having been disorganized.

Some forty or more years ago — I do not have the exact date — a Methodist Church was formed in the town, which held regular meetings for a time, but it had a short life, as it did not find the place an encouraging field of labor.

A Baptist Church was formed at East Bluehill in recent times, and they have a fine church edifice sufficient and suitable for their requirements.

The foregoing is a mere outline of the church history of the town, which, it is to be hoped, may be filled in and enlarged upon at a future time.

The work of the churches, with the academy, has exerted a great influence in forming the mental, moral, and religious character and standing of the people of the town.

But the work of the district schools should not be omitted in mentioning the agencies that have been important in moulding the character and in elevating the condition of the people. The early settlers were aware of the benefits to be derived from a system of training their children in the elementary branches of education, and so we find that early in the history of the town they appropriated money to hire teachers, to build school houses, and to firmly establish the common school system in the town. I, for one, have great respect for their wisdom and forethought in this matter. The work done in the " *little red school-houses* " of the town and of the country has never received that full share of commendation to which it is entitled. I have great respect for the " *little red school-houses* " — and I am sorry to see that a change has been made in the color of their paint in later years — for there was laid for me the foundation of what little education I possess, and through them, and by what I received from the academy, I have been enabled to accomplish in life whatever I have done worth accomplishing.

I bring to mind the days when Father Fisher was one of the school committee, and I a boy in the school, and how I was instructed to take off my hat and make my manners to him when we met on the street. Yes, and I bring to mind, too, the flogging I received from a school teacher. You older persons present will remember that flogging was deemed to be as necessary a part of every well-regulated school as the course of study, and perhaps more so. I then thought that the punishment I received was unjust, and maturer years and judgment have failed to work in me an opposite opinion. I mentally resolved that when I should be large enough I would thrash him in return if a favorable opportunity offered. In 1850, I drove one day from the Falls to the village, and on the way overtook and invited my old teacher to ride with me, and he accepted. When comfortably seated by my side, I asked if he knew me; he said he did not. I told him my name, that I went to school to him, that he thrashed me as I thought without just cause. The old man said he did not remember anything about it, which I readily believed, for he had flogged hundreds of boys and girls in his day. I said to him, "I promised myself to thrash you when I should be large enough to do it:"—the old man grew uneasy in his seat. I said, "I am now large and strong enough to flog a dozen men of your age and infirmities, but don't be in the least alarmed, I shall not harm a hair of your head." The old gentleman felt at ease after that, and we had a pleasant chat the rest of the way to the village, where we parted never to meet again in this life.

He was a type of the old-time school-master, of whom the boys and girls of the present day know nothing by their own experience; and it is well they do not, for it was a hard and difficult task to flog intelligence into the brains of the ordinary child of those days.

An incident was related to me some years ago, which illustrated the character of the people of Bluehill a hundred years ago or less. At that time Hancock County comprised not only its present territory, but what is now Waldo and Penobscot Counties. A sheriff came to Bluehill to arrest one of its inhabitants and lodge him in jail for debt. The citizens learned what his errand was, and gathered together to talk the matter over. They discussed the matter, and agreed that to have one of their townsmen arrested and put in jail for debt would be a lasting disgrace to the town. The result was that they raised among themselves the amount of the debt, paid it over to the sheriff, and saved the good name of their townsman, and preserved the honor of the town. These men who exhibited such a high regard for the honor and good name of their town, were part of the early settlers, in whose honor we are met to-day, and in whom we feel a just pride.

The early settlers and their descendants, notwithstanding their zealous care for church and state, did not relax their energies in the direction of subduing the forests, clearing and cultivating the soil, erecting dwellings and barns from time to time as their needs required, which brought the town to the prosperous condition in which we behold it to-day. They not only did that, but they did more; they erected saw and grist mills, built, manned, and freighted fleets of vessels,*

---

* It is recorded that on January 23, 1768, "Capt. Russ sailed for the West Indies, being the first who ever sailed from this place for that part of the world." The cargo of his vessel was lumber, no doubt; but what the name of his vessel was, her size, rig, &c., and where she and Capt. Russ hailed from, we do not know.

opened up and worked quarries of granite, from which have been taken stone to be erected into imposing structures, that now beautify and adorn many of the cities of our land; built, fitted out, and manned fleets of fishing vessels, and displayed an energy and perseverance in these undertakings worthy of the success they have achieved. We should expect the children of such parentage to inherit the activities and tendencies of their sires, and improve upon the foundations laid for them, and we are not disappointed in that respect. Of the mining interests of the town I am not prepared to speak at this time; they are too recent to take up any part of our attention for to-day.

The sons and daughters of Bluehill, and of other towns in Maine, have not only won for themselves honorable mention at home, but they are to be found as citizens of different States,* from the Atlantic to the Pacific and from the North Eastern boundary of Maine to Texas, and, by their sturdy energies and their honesty of character, have helped to mold our modern civilization and to build up our great country. They, like the early settlers of this region, have sought for themselves homes far removed from their ancestral hearth-stones, and have carried with them the principles which were here taught them, and have exerted an influence

---

* W. Preston Wood, a descendant of Joseph Wood, of the fifth generation, and Mabel (Candage) Wood, his wife, a descendant of John Roundy, of the fifth generation, are now residents of Orange Park, Florida.

for good which has not been lost to the country at large.

"A good name," said Solomon, "is rather to be desired than great riches"; and the man, be he old or young, who wins for himself a name for honest, moral worth, and for upright Christian character, gains a noble position for himself, and a large legacy for his posterity, though he may possess very little of this world's goods.

Not many of the descendants of this town have won *great distinction and honors* among their fellow-men, nor was it to be expected they would. It is the mass that make a state, a country, and a nation. There are few towering intellects and leaders in a community of educated, intelligent people. But it is a great gain to every community to be educated and intelligent. A few, however, have acquired honors and distinction, who are descended from the people of this town; for instance, the present Chief Justice of the Supreme Court of this State, Hon. John A. Peters, whose father was born here, and whose grandfather was a man of mark, and highly respected among the first settlers. And there are others who might be mentioned, if time would permit.

Our ancestors had respect for character, and so should we; and they could not have expressed it in a stronger way than they did, when they voted " to hire a person to preach the Gospel to us, in order that their children should not grow up like the heathen. "

I am aware that there is a tendency among those

claiming to represent Young America at the present time, to characterize the teachings of our forefathers as "old fogyism." But it will be a sad day for this country and for the world, when the teachings of the Sermon on the Mount and of the Gospel are outgrown.

The citizens of Bluehill, among their other characteristics, have never been lacking in patriotism and in love of country. Christopher Osgood, one of its first settlers, was a soldier in the Revolutionary army at the battle of Bunker Hill, and another, Nehemiah Hinckley, served through the war, and was honorably discharged at West Point at its close. Col. Nathan Parker was an officer in the Provincial army at the siege and fall of Louisburg. A number were in the service during the war with great Britain in 1812-15; and Mr. Crockett, who formerly lived on the Neck, was impressed on board a British man-of-war, where he was made to serve against his will; and it is to the credit of the town that when there was likely to be a war with Great Britain, respecting the North Eastern Boundary dispute, a large number went to the Aroostook to defend the territory of their State from invasion and spoliation.

John Arnold, a citizen of the town, was engaged in the field during the Mexican war, and several were engaged in the transport service in aid of that war.

In the great Civil War of 1861–65, the people of Bluehill were loyal to the cause of the Union, and did good service on land and sea in putting down the Rebellion. A more honorable record than that of the citizens of this town was not made any where. The Gazetteer of Maine states that Bluehill furnished 196 men in defence of the Union, and paid out in bounties to the enlisted men some $18,000 in money! I feel a just sense of pride in my native place as I rehearse to you the honorable part her citizens have taken to defend their country from the assaults of foreign and domestic foes. And I feel a pride in her people, who, by their energy and perseverance, caused to be cut by a citizen of the town, from a native block of granite, the beautiful and appropriate monument which has been set up in yonder cemetery in memory of those brave men from Bluehill, who laid down their lives for their country! I feel I ought to bare my head as I pass it, out of respect for the men whose death it commemorates, for the deeds of daring and of valor performed by them and by their comrades still living, of which it speaks to every beholder, in language mute, but full of eloquence and pathos.

It is well we have gathered here to-day to study the history of our town, and the lives and characters of our townsmen, — what they did for us, what examples they set us, and how we may profit by them.

It is well for us, and especially so for the young, to be taught by a review of the historical events which we have so briefly recounted, that service for others is honorable and elevating; that the greatest benefactors have been those, who, without expectation of reward, have performed the greatest service; that honest toil, even when those who come after us shall reap its benefits, is not degrading, but is manly, and will bring a sure reward.

The centennial anniversary of the town's incorporation will occur on the 30th of January, 1889, a little more than two years hence, and it is to be hoped that arrangements will early be effected to celebrate it in an appropriate and becoming manner. I trust, too, that measures will be taken to have a history of the town published, for which there are abundant materials and talent to carry forward the work; but it requires money to meet the expense of publication, which must be raised in some way. I think I could name the person who would be willing to undertake its publication, provided proper aid and support should be given him. It is also to be hoped that the citizens will be aroused to aid in the work, by the gathering together of family histories and biographies, and other interesting matter in regard to the early settlers, and the progress made by the community, which, if neglected, would in a few years be lost, but which can now be collected and preserved.

It would be a commendable undertaking for the persons gathered here to form themselves into the Bluehill Historical Society, having for its purpose the collection and preservation of all historical matter bearing upon the settlement and progress of the town and vicinity, and to provide a place of safe deposit for the same.

In furtherance of these suggestions, let me ask, why an annual clam-bake, of which this may be called the first, should not be held on this spot, at which the citizens of Bluehill and vicinity may assemble, and spend a day of profit and pleasure together.

And now, what has been to me a pleasing task is finished. I regret for your sakes, however, that it did not fall to the lot of one more able and better equipped for the work.

Every one who has had experience in culling historical data for his use, has encountered difficulty in deciding what to select and what to reject, and such has been my case.

If, however, this shall prove to be the means of awakening you to a deeper interest in the matters touched upon, I shall feel well paid for the time and labor bestowed upon it.

Thanking you for the kind and considerate attention you have accorded to me, I close with renewed feelings of friendship for you all, with affection for my native town, with great respect for the lives and character of its founders, and with becoming pride in its history and in its historical associations.